How to Make Six Figures a Year: Jobs That Pay $100k With No Degree

By Tim Wiseman

How to Make Six Figures a Year: Jobs That Pay $100k With No Degree

© 2019 Tim Wiseman

All rights reserved.

No portion of this book may be reproduced in any form without permission from the author, except as permitted by U.S. copyright law.

Cover by James at Go On Write at
https://www.goonwrite.com

Dedicated to every person who believes they are worth more

Table on Contents

Introduction	5
Author's Note: About the Data	7
Air Traffic Controller	8
Artist	11
Author	15
Blogger	18
Car Salesman	22
Civil Servant	26
Construction Manager	32
Court Stenographer	35
Dental Hygienist	37
eBay Store Owner	39
Electrician	42
Elevator Technician	44
Film and Video Editor	46
Franchise Owner	49
Funeral Director	52
Information Technology Worker	55
Insurance Sales	57
Investigator	59
Loan Officer	61
Makeup Artist	64
Military	67
Nuclear Power Reactor Operator	71
Pilot	73
Police Officer	75
Plumber	77
Prison Guard	79
Radiation Therapist	82

Real Estate Appraiser	84
Real Estate Broker	86
Researcher	89
Sales Manager	93
Skycap	96
Small Business Owner	98
Tattoo Artist	101
UPS Driver	104
USPS Postal Worker	107
Waiter	111
Wedding Photographer	114
YouTube Entrepreneur	117

Introduction

Now, more than ever, students are questioning the value of spending years in college and incurring thousands of dollars of student loans – a gamble which may not pay off when they graduate. For example, the average starting salary of a new graduate in 2018 was $50,390. That sounds pretty good – until you realize many new graduates live in cities where the average apartment is over $2,000 a month, or a new graduate may have student loan repayment plans that are in excess of $500+ a month!

What if there was a way to earn six figures a year – or more – without getting a four-year degree?

There is.

I wrote this book to introduce you to a variety of six-figure careers that don't require a four-year college degree. That being said, some of the careers may require some college coursework, professional training, or certification.

If you're just starting out in your first career, or you're unemployed, or you need to retrain for a new career after being laid off or downsized, you will find many careers in this book that you can train for in two years or less.

Some of the careers in this book may surprise you. If you're looking for a non-traditional career path, some of these thinking-outside-the-box career options may help you to decide what direction to go in.

You will notice that the median annual wage of many of these jobs is less than $100,000. However, in order to qualify for selection for this book, the top 10% of earners in this field had to make $100,000 or more. That means that each position selected for this book has the *potential* to earn six-figures – and sometimes much more.

Good luck!

Author's Note: About the Data

This section is where I tell you where I got my data from.

I got all of the data from this book from the Bureau of Labor Statistic's *Occupational Outlook Handbook*.

This is the most authoritative and current source on salary information in the United States. It is produced by a branch of the United States government.

To verify the data in this book, just go to:
https://www.bls.gov/ooh

In a few instances where information could not be obtained from the *Occupational Outlook Handbook* (example: Small Business Owner, Franchise Owner) than other sources such as Payscale.com and Entrepreneur.com were used.

Air Traffic Controller

- Median yearly wage: $124,540
- **Top 10% of earners: $175,800**
- Typical education: Associate's degree
- Additional job requirements: Military experience, or a FAA-approved program, or a A.A. from a AT-CTI (Air Traffic Collegiate Training Initiative)

What the Job Entails:

Air traffic controllers monitor thousands of flights per day. They follow strict procedures to assure maximum safety and minimal delays for each individual flight.

Overall, they direct the movement of all flight traffic coming in and out of an airport. They are the ones who tell pilots when it is okay to take off, and when they can land. They inform pilots of the weather, potential weather problems, runway closures, delays, and other problems with landing or taking off. In case of an emergency, they alert airport emergency and medical staff.

Air traffic controllers work closely with computers, radars, and other technology to monitor flight paths and incoming/outgoing flights. They usually oversee the flow of several airplanes at once, and communicate with multiple staff at one time. They typically work from control towers and manage air traffic that is up to thirty miles away from the airport.

Air traffic controllers must have excellent technical and aeronautical skills. They work nights, weekends, and may have rotating shifts.

How to Get a Job:

There are many requirements to becoming an air traffic controller.

Air traffic controllers must:
- Be a U.S. citizen
- Be fluent in English
- Pass a medical evaluation
- Pass a background check
- Pass the FAA pre-employment test
- Pass the ATSA (Air Traffic Controller Specialist Skills Assessment Battery)
- Complete a training course at the FAA Academy
- Be under the age of 31

Once employed, air traffic controllers must pass a physical exam each year. They must also pass an employment exam twice a year, and periodic drug tests.

There are three paths to becoming an air traffic controller:
1. Have three years of progressively responsible work experience and some college from an AT-CTI program
2. Have an associate's degree from an AT-CTI program
3. Have a bachelor's degree from an AT-CTI program

Air traffic controllers are trained at the FAA Academy in Oklahoma. Applicants must be hired by their 31st birthday.

After completing their training, applicants begin their work as developmental controllers, until they complete all requirements and become a certified air traffic controller.

Artist

- Median yearly wage: $49,160
- **Top 10% of earners: $101,120**
- Typical education: High school degree or above
- Additional job requirements: None, although some choose to get a degree in Arts

What the Job Entails:

Many people aspire to be a professional artist: not only can it come with great financial perks, but it also bestows prestige, power, and a sense of transcendence.

Artists works in a variety of mediums: paint, drawing, jewelry, glass, computer graphics, etc.

Artists can be all of the following:
- Animator
- Cartoonist
- Comic book artist
- Fashion designer
- Glass blower
- Graphic artist
- Illustrator (Commercial, medical, or scientific)
- Jeweler
- Painter
- Potter
- Quilter
- Sculptor
- Stained glass artist
- Textile/Fiber artist

Many artists do not have formal training or an education. Many are so compelled to create art that they began long before the years in which they would begin a traditional education (they started creating art as a teen or a child, etc.) Many young people are so compelled to create art that they have their first showings before they finish high school!

Whether you've known since you were a child that you were made to create art, or you're a latecomer to the field, art is one of those careers where you are does not matter.

Artists may either work independently (such as a painter or jewelry designer) or as part of a team (animator, storyboard artist, print maker) to work an artistic project of great scale. They may take a project from inception to finish (creative idea, design, creation, finishing, exhibition) or work on one piece of it. Some artists also end up working in related fields of art, such as a museum curator, restoration artist, or gallery owner. Some artists also get second job teaching art in schools – whether at the elementary, high school, or college level. Some also supplement their income by giving art lessons or tutoring art students.

How to Get a Job:

As previously mentioned, formal credentials are not necessary. You can simply start creating art at any time, in any way you prefer!

There are many easy ways to break into the art field. You can start:
Selling your crafts on eBay
Selling your crafts on etsy
Sell artistic commissions on freelance websites, such as Fiverr

Book a booth at Artist's Alley at a comic book convention
Attend a community college art class and display your work in their student gallery
Contact local galleries with samples of your artwork
Ask local restaurants and businesses if they will display your artwork
Get listed in a local wedding magazine as a photographer
Sell street art at urban locations on Friday and Saturday nights
Set up an easel at a popular location (beach, farmer's market, outdoor event) and offer to do commissioned drawings

However, to get a position with a company as an artist – say, as an animator for Disney, a comic book artist for Marvel, as a graphic designer for a local company, or as an art teacher for a high school – you will most likely need educational credentials in addition to a sample portfolio of your work.

How much money can you make as an artist?

These are some sample salaries:
- San Francisco Academy of Art Instructor: $80,298
- Fashion Designer: $80,200
- Film editor at Pixar: $82,000
- Illustrator/Storyboarder: $91,200
- Interior Designer: $101,000
- Creative Director: $103,000
- Cartoonist/Animator at Disney: $116,000+

- Wedding Photographer: $156,000 (assuming $3,000 per wedding, 52 weeks/year)

Author

- Median yearly wage: $61,820
- **Top 10% of earners: $118,760**
- Typical education: High school degree
- Additional job requirements: None, although some choose to get Creative Writing or English degrees

What the Job Entails:

Authors *are* writers – and there are many different kind of writers.

Here are a few types:
- Biographers
- Bloggers (more on that in the next section)
- Copywriters
- Ghostwriters
- Novelists
- Playwrights
- Researchers
- Technical writers

Authors create written content for advertisers, magazines, books, blogs, websites, social media sites, movies, plays, television shows, and they also write novels, short stories, and poetry.

It is up to authors to write on subject matters that will engage, convince, or compel readers. For some writers, that means writing a creative or suspenseful novel. For others, it means writing a factual article or a corporate biography.

One of the biggest perks of writing is that many authors get to write from home.

Another enormous perk is that writers get to set their own work schedule. Early birds and night owls alike can typically write during their preferred hours. The only thing required to write is a pen and a pad of paper, or more commonly, a computer.

Many writers live in areas where there is a strong communications, entertainment, or publishing industry, such as Los Angeles or New York.

How to Get a Job:

Some authors choose to get degrees in English, Creative Writing, Journalism, or Communications. Degrees are not necessary, especially if your plan is to write fiction – many a high school graduate has gone on to writing success. Many people realize their natural affinity for writing when they join a high school or college weekly newspaper. From there, they may begin writing opinions, editorials, and small articles for newspapers and magazines.

Writers are typically self-employed, and expected to do their own marketing and promotion. At a minimum, you will need to be able to create your own website, social media presence, press releases, and newsletter. Writers often choose to have their own blogs and do guest blog posts on other writer's sites.

Most writers typical start by writing different pieces and either submitting them for publication or self-publishing them. Given the current state of the market, you can begin your writing career overnight. Simply start a blog or write a novella and self-publish it.

Blogger

- Median yearly wage: $1200
- **Top 10% of earners: $100,000+**
- Typical education: High school
- Additional job requirements: None, although you should be a subject expert

What the Job Entails:

Bloggers are a type of writers.

Blogging has been around since the late 1990's. It started as a type of online diary, where people would keep an ongoing account of the most interesting things that happened in their daily lives.

Blogging platforms increased the number and popularity of blogs. Some examples are: Open Diary, LiveJournal, Blogger, and WordPress.

Blogs can be on any subject: politics, cooking, food, crafts, pets, sports, hobbies, music, travel, etc.

Here are some ideas for blog topics to get you started:
- Anti-vaccination
- Autism/Autism awareness
- Beauty/Fashion
- Black Lives Matter
- Blog/How to start a really popular blog
- Brewing/Beer
- Cats (Especially if devoted to a certain breed)

- Childfree/Childless
- Credit Card Debt (How to Get Out of Debt…)
- Dating (For either gender)
- Dogs (Especially if devoted to a certain breed)
- Early Retirement (How to retire in your 30's, 40's, 50's)
- eBay/Hot eBay Finds/Selling on eBay
- Exercise
- Food Allergies
- Geographical Lifestyle (For big cities…Life in London…Life in the Big Apple…)
- Hair Dressing/Hair Updos
- How to Get Your Ex Back
- How to Get Over Your Ex
- Low Carb
- Men's Lifestyle/Alpha Male
- Millennials
- Paleo
- SAT Scores/How to get a perfect score on SAT
- Supplements
- Student Loan Debt (How to Get Out of Debt…)
- Travel
- TV Show (For fans of a particular TV show or series…)
- Vegan
- Video Games
- Wedding Planning
- Wine
- Women's Lifestyle

- YouTube/How to create a popular YouTube channel

So, how much can you earn blogging?

It depends on how hard you work at it and how much of a market you attract. Some people start blogs as a part-time job on top of their regular job, just to supplement their income. Some people work on their blogs more as a hobby, doing it just for fun. Others make it their full-time, professional job, treating it like a business.

Around 10% of bloggers earn nothing from their blogs. On the other hand, over 50% of bloggers earn at least some kind of income from their blog – from $1 - $99 a month. The top 10% of bloggers earn somewhere from between $1,000 – $10,000+ a month from their blog. The top 4% earn more than $10,000+ a month.

If your blog becomes wildly popular, you can sell it for a great deal of money. These are some tope blog sales:

Arseblog – sold for $5 million
Weblogs – sold for $25 million
TechCrunch – sold for $30 million
Ugo.com – sold for $100 million

How to Get a Job:

Starting a blog is incredibly simple. You can literally start one overnight.

To make your blog truly professional, you will want to register your own domain name. Don't go with a free blog name like: blognamehere.blogspot.com or blognamehere.wix.com

Your blog name should read as your name or whatever you site is about, like: sarahpeters.com or dailyrecipesin20minutes.com

You will need to register your domain name and then chose a blog site to host it.

You can use free graphic sites to create headers, logo, and pictures for your blog.

Your blog posts should have pictures whenever possible. Studies have found that people are 80% more likely to read something with a picture instead of just a straight block of text. Many websites offer free photos or photos through the Creative Commons License, as long as you site the source that it's from. You can also purchase a monthly subscription to a stock photo site.

You will need to keep your blog updated with regular content. Try to post daily, or at least several times a week.

Once you have a fan base visiting your site, you can have Google Ads places on the sidebars and footers of your site, which will help you generate income.

Car Salesman

- Median yearly wage: $45,000
- **Top 10% of earners: $100,000+**
- Typical education: High school
- Additional job requirements: None

What the Job Entails:

More than a million Americans work at car dealerships. Some of these people, typically the car salesmen (and women!) are rolling in the dough.

Some salesmen work entirely off commission. Some work off commission and hourly pay. Working strictly off of commission can be particularly intense, because if you sell nothing, you earn nothing! You aren't paid for standing around for 8 to 12 hours a day. On days that you sell nothing, this can feel like a total loss.

On the other end of the spectrum, many people have had very successful six-figure careers in selling cars.

How do you make six figures selling cars?

High-volume car salesmen typically sell 20 or more cars per month.

How much do they make? Commissions vary based on the type of car sold. The minimum commission on a sale tends to vary between $125 - $200. Most car salespeople average $330 per sale.

Commissions also vary based on whether the car is new or used. A new car may have a $330 commission. A used car, with a greater markup, may have a $1,000 commission. The profit margin is greater on used cars, many of which are bought at auction for pennies on the dollar.

What if you don't sell 20 cars a month? What if you sell less?

Salespeople typically have a quota of 8 to 12 cars per month. Salespeople who don't make the minimum quota rarely stick it out in the business. However, salespeople who regularly exceed their quota by 20% or more often see an increase in their base commission. Sell more cars, make more money.

Most salespeople average around 10 car sales per month. So in order to sell 20 cars a month, you need to learn to be a good sales person.

In addition to commission, car salespeople often get "spiffs." When a car is proving particularly hard to sell, some dealerships will offer a cash bonus, called a "spiff" to the car salesperson who gets it off the lot. These "spiff" bonuses can add up to an extra $5,000 to $10,000 a year.

Car salesmanship comes with a few downsides that should be addressed here. This career is not for everyone!

Be aware that this can be a cut-throat work environment! You and many other people are all competing to sell cars – someone else's win is *your* loss. Don't expect to be great buddies with your coworkers.

Car salesmen are disliked. Just try telling other people at a party what you do, and see how warm of a reception you get. Car salesmen are consistently ranked in Gallup polls as being one of the most dishonest, unethical professions in America. People like car salesmen about as much as they like bill collections, politicians, and lawyers.

How to Get a Job:

The hardest part of getting a job at a car dealership is passing the sales interview. You don't need an education, or previous work experience, or to know someone. You just need to be able to convince the manager to take a chance on you – and then succeed.

The sales interview will be your first test. This isn't a nice, sit-down interview where you answer questions about your work experience and how well you work as a team player.

Typically, it is the Sales Manager conducts the interview. He (or she) will want to see some live, immediate selling skills from you. He (or she) may take you out onto the lot and have you pretend that they are a customer. You will need to try to sell them a car. This is a pass/fail exercise.

If you don't have experience selling cars, don't worry. Many Sales Managers like to hire people who have never worked in sales before. That way, they can train the newbie in exactly the way that they prefer. Many dealerships like to hire people straight out of high school.

During the interview, ask questions about the commission structure, hourly rate (if there is one), dealership pay structure, and bonuses.

And don't be disappointed if you don't see a car on your first day.

Civil Servant

- Median yearly wage: $88,809
- **Top 10% of earners: $123,160**
- Typical education: High school degree
- Additional job requirements: College can result in a higher wage

What the Job Entails:

The federal government is the largest employer in the nation. Altogether, they employ around 2.7 million people.

The city, county, and state governments employ million more.

All told, around 1 in 5 Americans work for the government.

Although most of the information here is listed for the federal government, you will find that this information also applies to any level of employment you are seeking – whether it's city, county, or state. Government employment is the same no matter where. It has the same generous benefits, the same civil service testing process, the same sort of pay scales. Many government employees switch between city, county, state, and federal employment through their lifetime.

So, what exactly does the federal government do? It:
- Defends the United States from foreign aggression and terrorism
- Represent U.S. interests abroad

- Enforce laws and regulations
- Administer domestic programs and agencies

The federal government is composed of over 100 independent agencies and 15 Cabinet departments. Each agency has a headquarters, typically located in Washington D.C., with regional offices around the country.

A little less than 15% of federal employees worked in or around Washington D.C.. About 3% are assigned overseas

Why do people want a federal job? Commonly cited reasons are:
- Job security
- Good pay
- Excellent retirement
- Nationwide and overseas job opportunities

Once you are employed by the government and you have passed probation, you have a job for life.

One of the reasons why people are so eager to work for the government is because of the excellent benefits. For example, the insurance. When you work for the federal government, you get access to the following insurance packages:
- FEGLI – Federal Employee's Group Life Insurance
- FEHB – Federal Employees Health Benefits
- FEDVIP – Federal Employees Dental & Vision Insurance Program

The federal government also offers two retirement plans:
- FERS – Federal Employees Retirement System
- TSP – Thrift Savings Plan – 401k

Overall, the average benefits package for a federal employee exceeds $41,000 a year!

What about actual pay?

Workers are paid under the (GS) General Schedule pay scale. There are 15 grades of pay for workers.

People who are just starting at the lowest levels of government service, such as a Food Service Worker, Custodian, Typist, or Office Clerk, will start at GS 1 or 2.

High school graduates usually begin at the GS 2 level. Graduates with Associate degrees typically start at GS-4. Bachelor's degrees typically start at GS-5 to GS-7. PhD's typically start at the GS-9 to GS-11 level.

However, you don't *need* a college education to reach these high GS levels. Many people start at the bottom and work their way up over the years, qualifying for high GS levels on the basis of their experience, and not education. 55% of federal workers do not have a college degree

So, how high can the pay get?

GS 13 will get you up to $98,317 a year.

GS 14 will get you up to $116,181 a year.

GS 15 will get you up to $136,659 a year.

Your pay can also be increased depending on where in the country you live. Federal employees in the U.S. receive locality pay – pay based on surveys against local pay in the geographical area. For example, if you live in San Francisco or New York City, your pay will be higher than if you lived in a small, rural town.

The government is a favorite employer for veterans. Over 30% of federal employees are veterans. Veterans who have been honorably or medically discharged can apply for. Veteran's Preference Points. These increase your exam score by several points, giving you a better exam score. These are not "free" or "giveaway" points – these

Government jobs are also a great fit for the disabled. For those who are disabled, they must provide proof of either:
- A severe physical disability
- A psychiatric disability
- An intellectual disability

A doctor, licensed medical professional, or licensed vocational rehabilitation specialist may write the letter documenting a candidate's disability. Agencies will also accept a letter from any federal, state, or local agency that issues or provides disability benefits

Disabled persons go through a noncompetitive process for employment.

How to Get a Job:

How do you get a civil service job?

Civil service means that you are hired by your merit and skills. You cannot have preferential hiring, favoritism, or nepotism in civil service hiring.

To become a civil servant, you must do three things:
1. Show evidence of appropriate education and experience for the job
2. Show evidence of having the skills required for the job
3. Pass a civil-service examination specifically for the job

Applicants must be U.S. citizens.

Whether you are applying for a city, county, state, or federal job, you will need to create an online account for whatever local area of government it is. For the federal level, you can create an account at: www.usajobs.gov

To apply for a position, you will either need to take an exam, or submit evidence that you are qualified for that position. About 20% of civil service positions still involve formal exams. Civil service exams are rated on a scale of 100, with 70 and above usually considered "passing."

These exams are rated by the agency doing the hiring. The rest of government jobs are filled through an analysis of your background, work experience, and education – not through a written exam.

For jobs involving classified or sensitive materials, applicants must undergo a background investigation in order to get security clearance. Their criminal records, credit records, and employment history will be checked.

Construction Manager

- Median yearly wage: $91,370
- **Top 10% of earners: $159,560**
- Typical education: High school diploma; on-the-job training
- Additional job requirements: Licensing

What the Job Entails:

Construction managers - much like it sounds - manage constructions sites or projects.

This can involve far-reaching work. Projects typically begin with a cost estimate and a budget, and construction managers oversee the project to its final completion. Along the way, they most work closely with other building professionals and ensure that the project comes in on time and on budget.

They typically start a job by preparing cost estimates, a budget, and work timetables. They draw up a contract for the work and convey the technical information about the project to other members of the team and contracted professionals. They serve as a liaison between the person who originated the contract (client) and the professionals who are working on the project. They are responsible for the project – and that means solving problems, too. Construction managers deal with work delays, emergencies, scheduling issues, complying with legal codes and regulations, and supervising workers.

As the project progresses, they report on the work and budget to the client. They work closely with architects, engineers, subcontractors, stonemasons, electricians, carpenters, civil engineers, lawyers, government officials, and other specialists.

Construction managers may work on a variety of projects, depending on their specialty. That could mean any of the following: public, residential, commercial, industrial, warehouses, roads, memorials, bridges, urban projects, convention centers, municipal buildings, apartment buildings.

How to Get a Job:

Many construction managers have degrees, as there are several schools now offering degrees in Construction Management.

However, many construction managers get by on work experience alone, provided that they can show they have skills and experience in such topics as:
- Structural design
- Building codes
- Construction scheduling
- Environmental science
- Landscaping
- Engineering
- Architecture
- Safety management
- Project management

- Concrete and construction
- Business law
- Materials
- Carpentry
- Masonry

Managers typically acquire their skills through on-the-job training. Large construction firms will typically prefer candidates who have degrees; small construction firms, family-owned firms, and minority-owned firms are more likely to take you on and give you the on-the-job experience you need.

New construction managers are typically hired as assistants and may train or apprentice under an experienced construction managers for several years.

Some states require licensure for construction managers – check with your state licensing board. You may have to become licensed through a local government agency, or produce a certificate from an accredited association, like the Construction Management Association of America or the American Institute of Constructors.

Court Stenographer

- Median yearly wage: $,120
- **Top 10% of earners: $100,270**
- Typical education: Certificate
- Additional job requirements: Licensing

What the Job Entails:

Court reporters may seem to have a mysterious job. Most people have never encountered one unless they've been on the inside of a courtroom.

Court reporters listen and type simultaneously at enormous speeds, creating a word-for-word (verbatim) transcript of the spoken word. They are typically found in courtrooms – at depositions, hearings, proceedings, or legal events.

Not only may they record word-for-word dialogue, but they may also record who is speaking, their gestures, and their actions. They may ask for clarification when the speaker is too soft or unintelligible. If required, they may repeat back dialogue for the judge. Their notes become the transcripts that are provided to the courts, counsel, media, and public.

How to Get a Job:

Most states require you to take a high-speed typing test and pass a licensing exam.

Some states require you to be a member of a professional association. These would be associations such as the National Court Reporters Association, United States Court Reporters Association, American Association of Electronic Reporters and Transcribers, National Verbatim Reporters Association, or a state-level Court Reporters Association.

Court reporters typically receive their training at a community college or technical school. These programs issue a certificate or an A.A. degree. Education is likely to be concentrated on subjects such as phonetics, the English language, typing, and legal terminology and vocabulary.

Dental Hygienist

- Median yearly wage: $74,070
- **Top 10% of earners: $101,330**
- Typical education:
- Additional job requirements: Licensing

What the Job Entails:

They clean teeth, remove tarter and stains, look for signs of dental disease (gingivitis, etc.), take x-rays, apply fluoride, keep patient's dental charts and records, and assist the dentist in filling cavities, bridges, crowns, etc. They also are usually the first face that a patient sees when they enter the back end of a dental office, and they help prepare the patient for more complicated procedures being done by the dentist.

Dental hygienists have a one-on-one relationship with their patients. They teach clients about good oral health, including the proper way to brush and floss, and recommend different mouthwashes, toothpastes, etc.

Dental hygienists should be calm, good with people, have excellent fine motor skills,a nd ebe good with working in small spaces.

How to Get a Job:

The typical education for a dental hygienist is an A.A. degree or a training program. Some older dental hygienists learned through a program administered in high school, or a one-year training program.

Programs in dental hygiene are taught in technical schools and community colleges. Students learn the basics of:
- Periodontics
- Patient management
- Record keeping
- Radiography
- Pathology
- Medical ethics

There is also a lab component and an apprenticeship.

All states require that their dental hygienists be licensed. Constant your state's Board of Dental Examiners.

eBay Store Owner

- Median yearly wage: $100,000+
- **Top 10% of earners: $500,000+**
- Typical education: None
- Additional job requirements: None

What the Job Entails:

Selling on eBay is pretty simple. You put items – new or used – up for sale on eBay, either as a fixed-price listing or an auction listing. A fixed-price listing is when you set the price that you are willing to sell the item at – that price, and only that price. An auction is when you list it, usually at a pretty low price, and then hope that a large number of potential buyers become interested in your item and bid the price up to be very high.

Where do you acquire items to sell on eBay? Most people start by looking for items around their house. From there, they may begin asking friends for items that they no longer want and plan on giving to a thrift store. Many sellers then begin thrifting, going to yard sales, and attending auctions. Some apply for a wholesaler license so that they can purchase large lots of items and then sell them on eBay.

One of the most famous eBay sellers is Linda Lightman, who makes $25 million a year selling on eBay. She began by selling her son's video games. Once she ran out of video games, she started selling her own clothes, shoes, and accessories. After that, friends began asking her to sell their clothing. After a few years, she had warehouse space and over 20 employees, leading to a $25 million-a-year business.

About 1/3 of eBay sellers make under $10,000 a year. The next 1/3 make between $10,000 - $100,000 a year. The last 1/3 makes between $100,000 - $1 million a year. And the top 3.9% of eBay sellers make over $1 million per year.

How to Get a Job:

To sell on eBay, you just need to create an account on the website, and also sign up for a Paypal account. After that, you can begin listing!

When you are new on eBay, you will have 0 positive ratings. Buyers will be hesitant to purchase from you, because they do not yet know if you are a good and trustworthy seller yet. Expect to start off slow and gain more traction as you get more positive feedback. As of this writing, you can list up to 50 items for free on eBay. After that, you will pay a $0.35 fee for every item you list. Apps such as SaleCalc can help you determine how much of a profit you will be making before you ever list an item.

After you have proven that you provide consistent, well-performing listings, eBay will offer you Power Seller status.

Power Sellers qualify after:
- $3,000 in sales in the previous year
- 100 transactions in the past year with feedback at 98%+
- No more than .5% of transactions disputed by buyers

- eBay account in good standing with policy compliance

Power Sellers get a special icon with their listing letting buyers know of their special status as trusted sellers, and they also receive discounts on the fees they pay.

Electrician

- Median yearly wage: $54,110
- **Top 10% of earners: $92,690 (more when working nights, evenings, weekends)**
- Typical education: High school diploma
- Additional job requirements: Licensing

What the Job Entails:

Electricians work with power. They main install, repair, and do the maintenance of electrical system and control systems. They may work lights, appliances, and equipment. They may work in residential areas, businesses, factories, or industrial sites. They install wiring, electronical control, and lighting systems. They inspect and repair circuit breakers, outlets, wiring, fixtures, and work with voltage and amps. They must also insure that electrical systems meet safety and code requirements.

The most well-known plumbers are residential ones. They are called out to the home when the toilet and/or other pipe systems stop working or back up. Plumbers typically work nights, evenings, and weekends – and they charge additional fees for working these non-typical hours.

In particular, electricians need skills related to:
- Circuitry
- Electrical information
- Safety

How to Get a Job:

Most electricians do not have a formal education in their trade; instead, they learn through an apprenticeship. However, there are trade schools that offer an electrician education.

Apprentices are paid as they learn, getting about 2,000 hours of paid on-the-job training each year. They learn electrical theory, electrical code requirements, and safety practices. They begin as helpers and assistants, and gain more responsibility as they gain more experience.

To be employed as an apprentice, you must typically meet the following requirements:
- Be at least 18 years old
- Have a high school diploma or a GED
- Be physically fit
- Read, write, and comprehend English
- Must have a valid driver's license
- Be able to present the legal right to work in the United States
- Be able to attend class at least 2 nights a week and perform 2,000 on-the-job hours per year

After completing the apprenticeship program, workers are they promoted to the journey level. That means that they can work on their own.

Most states require plumbers to have a license and pass an exam demonstrating their knowledge of local and national electric and safety codes.

Elevator Technician

- Median yearly wage: $79,480
- **Top 10% of earners: $115,880**
- Typical education: High school diploma or equivalent
- Additional job requirements:

What the Job Entails:

Elevator technicians are crucial in order to keep modern buildings working. The average skyscraper has at least 40 floors; the tallest skyscrapers have over 100 floors. Having elevators that are safe, working, and running are necessary to keep these buildings running efficiently.

Technicians repair electrical wiring to control panels and motors, install new equipment, troubleshoot brakes, motors, switches, and controls. They repair elevators when things go wrong, such as emergency repairs – and they also do preventative maintenance. Their jobs also require that they follow national and state regulated building codes and safety regulations.

They also do preventative maintenance and insect elevators to ensure the safety of passengers and maintain compliance of safety regulations and building codes.

Elevator technicians either work alone or as part of a service crew team.

How to Get a Job:

Elevator technicians learn via apprenticeship.

Apprenticeship programs are about 4 years long. Apprentices have 2,000 hours of on-the-job training and 144 hours of technical instruction. During their training, apprentices learn about elevator and escalator parts, electrical theory, electronics, blueprint reading, and safety. Elevator technicians need a good understanding of electronics, hydraulics, and electricity.

Once apprentices have completed the program, they become assistant mechanics and mechanics.

Many states require licensure from the National Association of Elevator Contractors.

Elevator technicians who want to take their career further can also become certified as Qualified Elevator Inspectors by the National Association of Elevator Safety Authorities.

An additional unspoken requirement of the position is that technicians must be comfortable in small, confined, dark spaces. This is not a position for someone who is claustrophobic. Elevator technicians should also be physically fit, as they need to be able to fit into those small spaces, and they frequently need to move or haul heavy equipment.

Film and Video Editor

- Median yearly wage: $53,550
- **Top 10% of earners: $102,980**
- Typical education:
- Additional job requirements:

What the Job Entails:

Film and video editors create the raw and finished material that you see on television or an internet broadcast. They take raw footage and edit it into a finished product, based on the director's vision, the requirements of the parent company, or the required time slot of the finish product. They may shoot footage, but mostly they edit, cut, and compile scenes.

Editors may work on TV shows, movies, documentaries, music videos, sporting events, with news stations, or social media/websites/tech sites. They may also run their own small businesses. One person may choose to run their own wedding filming business, providing couples with a 20-minute highlight film of their wedding, while another may choose to be one of a crew employed by a major broadcasting network.

Almost all film and video editing work is done with computer software, so you must be skilled with technology and computers. Previous experience with video-editing software is helpful.

How to Get a Job:

Many film and video editors have a degree from an art college. However, this is still one of the careers where you can get by with a combination of education and experience, or just exceptional skills. Many editors are also "grandfathered" into these positions.

It is still possible to find positions that offer on-the-job training. If you already have experience with digital cameras and doing your own editing at home, you can build a portfolio to showcase to a potential employer.

Many editors self-educate through courses on YouTube, through Coursera, and through the Help features of editing software.

To get a position, you will need to be able to demonstrate that you are comfortable working with digital cameras and digital footage, use a variety of editing and audio software, transform raw footage into edited content and take it all the way through the postproduction phase, and show appropriate judgment and justification for the content you cut.

If you are going to be working as part of a team, you need to be able to demonstrate that you can work with producers, directors, journalists, and other editors in order to create a finished product that everyone is satisfied with.

A good way to start is to build an online portfolio of your work for potential employers to access. You may also try uploading your work across YouTube and popular social media sites to create a following and create fans of your work.

Franchise Owner

- Median yearly wage: $82,033
- Top 10% of earners: **$200,000+**
- Typical education: High school diploma or equivalent
- Additional job requirements: Business experience

What the Job Entails:

The owner of a franchise, also called a franchise, is someone who owns and operates a business that is part of a nationwide chain. These are most often fast food restaurants; think Baskin Robins, McDonalds, Subway, Krispy Kreme, Taco Bell, Pizza Hut, Wendy's, and 7-11.

The franchisee gets the right to use the name, trademark, product, and systems of the national business – in other words, they get the right to the brand. Other than that, the franchisee still has all the responsibilities and work that a small business owner has.

Why do people buy franchises, rather than starting their own small business? It's because you get an instant customer base, brand recognition, and support from the parent company. There is already an existing business model and a product – you just need to make the business run. On the downside, the parent company may have strict rules, regulations, and methods of product promotion and pricing that you are obligated to follow.

As a franchisee owner, you will likely have to work on the "front line" helping customers and making the food product, as well as acting as the boss. That means hiring and firing, training new staff, dealing with customer complaints, promoting your business, and filling in when no one else is available.

How to Get a Job:

Buying a franchise means that you will instantly become a small business owner. That doesn't mean that you need to have previous small business experience or have taken college classes in small business, but you should at least be aware of and comfortable with what owning a franchise entails.

Before buying a franchise, you should read *The Federal Trade Commission's Guide to Buying a Franchise.*

You might also investigate legitimate information sources on franchises, such as The International Franchising Association and The American Association of Franchisees.

The minimum requirements for owning a franchise is the ability to pay. You will need to pay the franchise fee and the cost of equipment. Before purchasing, you should read the Franchise Disclosure Document, which lists all of the information and business numbers on the potential franchise that you are looking to buy. If you are not familiar with all of the material, ask an accountant to review it with you.

To truly get to understand the franchise you are looking into purchasing, work at the business first. Many stores will only sell to franchisees who have worked their way up in the business, anyway. For example, Domino's gives preference to franchise applicants who have delivered pizzas and already worked on their stores; Dutch Brothers franchise applicants must have worked at the coffee shop for at least three years before they can buy.

Expect to spend at least $40,000 - $60,000 on the franchise fee – and sometimes much more. You should also expect to work diligently for the first few years to establish your business – and expect that you will be working a lot of nights and weekends!

Funeral Director

- Median yearly wage: $78,040
- Top 10% of earners: **$153,340**
- Typical education: Some college; A.A. degree
- Additional job requirements: Licensing

What the Job Entails:

Funeral directors typically have previous experience as a funeral service worker: a funeral assistant, attendant, mortician, receptionist, groundskeeper, etc. As they gain more experience, they can rise to the level of director.

Funeral service workers work closely with the family of a deceased person to determine the time, location, and manner of the visitation, reception, burial, or cremation. The record and implement all the details surrounding the burial: any religious customs to be observed, special handling of the body, helping organize the wake or memorial, and ensuring that the body appears in an appropriate state for the final service (embalmed, cremated and contained in an urn, etc.)

One of their most important roles is to act as a guide and a resource for bereaved families, who may be too overwhelmed to handle all of the details. They may recommend or contact chaplains, priests, florists, and related services. They provide information on all of the different funeral service options available – with a variety of options for different budgets. They collect the information for the headstone or tombstone, and produce the funeral announcements. They may help the family prepare and run an obituary.

They also deal with the body – transporting the remains, preparing it (embalming, cremating), and managing the paperwork associated with death. They help with the death certificate, and may help the family manage the paperwork associated with insurance, pensions, or death benefits.

The funeral director is responsible for overseeing the complete details of the funeral. These would be details such as: the opening and closing of the grave, installing the urn in the crematory, preparing for the shipment of the body, arranging for pallbearers and clergy service, and ensuring all of the appropriate paperwork is filed.

How to Get a Job:

Most funeral directors now have a two-year degree; some applicants may be "grandfathered" in.

Many community colleges offer courses for funeral service workers, with classes on ethics, business law, and embalming and restorative techniques.

You will also need to complete an internship or apprenticeship under a licensed funeral director.

Licensing laws and exams vary by state. Most states require you to pass a state or national board exam and be licensed to hold funeral services in the state where you work.

More information can be found with the National Funeral Directors Association, the Cremation Association of North America, and the International Cemetery, Cremation, and Funeral Association.

Information Technology Worker

- Median yearly wage: $81,100
- Top 10% of earners: **$130,200**
- Typical education: Some college, licensing and classes
- Additional job requirements: Certifications

What the Job Entails:

The definition of an information technology worker changes as often as the technology. These workers, depending on what they do, are called by several names: Information Security Analysts, Information Security Knowledge Worker, Information Technician, Computer Network Technician, Computer Systems Administrators.

Their job responsibilities vary. They may work with security in order to ensure that a company's computer networks are protected from cyberattacks. They may assist with the day-to-day operation of networks. They may develop and help with the maintenance of software applications. They may be responsible for various computer hardware. They may work as part of a held desk, directly helping internal staff or external users with troubleshooting.

They may work in small businesses, with entrepreneurs, or large companies. They may be part of a multi-national network, a small firm, or work from home. The information technology has limitless scope and opportunities.

How to Get a Job:

In the 1990's and early 2000's, very little was required to get a computer job. There were – and still are – many paths to working in the IT field. It is still possible to get into the IT field without a four-year degree in Computer Science. Many people are grandfathered in with their knowledge, experience, or exceptional skills.

Classes, certificates, or some college may be enough to gain an entry-level position. Since technology changes so rapidly, many employees accept certificates, seminars, and courses in recent technology. Many vendors also offer courses in their programs or software. Programming, technical, and software experience will go far here.

Once employed, you must have a commitment to continually refreshing and updating your skills. Technological advances occur so rapidly that you must continually study and update your certifications to remain competitive in this field.

Insurance Sales

- Median yearly wage: $49,710
- Top 10% of earners: **$125,190**
- Typical education: High school
- Additional job requirements: None

What the Job Entails:

Much like it sounds, those in insurance sales typically sell insurance. They may also be called Insurance Sales Agents.

Insurance sales agents are fluent in the different types of insurance, and sell this insurance directly to consumers or companies.

They typically meet one-on-one with clients. Some travel may be required.

Insurance sales agent typically must cold call, or convince customers that insurance is a needed product. They are in charge of expanding their own customer base and gaining new clients. That means they may do a lot of telephoning, emailing, or visiting different businesses to talk about insurance. They assess a client's needs, determine what insurance product would best suit them, explain the features of the insurance, and help them decide to purchase an insurance package.

Insurance Sales Agents must be comfortable with public speaking, cold calling, interacting with new people, and networking.

How to Get a Job:

Insurance sales agents don't need above a high school diploma. They do need a license in the state in which they work. The licenses they need may vary depending on whether they sell casualty insurance, life insurance, property insurance, and health insurance.

As an agent, you may also need to take continuing education courses or exams to keep up your license.

About half of all insurance agents work for companies that sell insurance, such as: AAA, Allstate, Farmers, Geico, etc. About one-quarter of all insurance agents are self-employed, getting commission on selling different insurance packages. The rest work directly for insurance and medical insurance carriers.

You can start your career by getting any position with a local insurance carrier – most of them have low-level positions in data entry or a call center, and then expressing your interest in becoming an insurance agent from there. Many companies have their own training and promotion programs for employees interested in working in sales.

Investigator

- Median yearly wage: $50,700
- Top 10% of earners: **$86,730 ($100,000+ with billable overtime)**
- Typical education: High school diploma
- Additional job requirements: N/A

What the Job Entails:

Being a private investigator is one of the more exciting jobs listed in this book.

The Bureau of Labor Statistic's Occupational Outlook Handbook cites the top 10% of investigators as earning $86k, but other news sources suggest that the salary goes as high as $125k a year – especially if you are self-employed or have billable overtime.

These are the things that private investigators may do:
- Perform background checks
- Check for criminal history
- Investigate theft
- Investigate fraud
- Conduct surveillance
- Remote or discreet surveillance
- Collect evidence
- Reconstruct crime or accident scenes
- Follow suspicious persons
- Proving infidelity in a marriage

Private investigation involves a lot of travel. You may follow persons from their home, to their office, to anywhere in between. And you need to stay hidden or discreet, while doing it.

Investigators may also specialize in locating missing persons or missing objects, like a car that needs to be repossessed or a person that needs to be served with legal papers. They may also help locate people for debt collection.

Sadly, some investigators also specialize in locating people for their families. In these scenarios, the person usually has fallen into drugs or addiction, and their whereabouts or unknown. This investigator will search for them so that they can be reunited with their family and receive professional help and treatment.

How to Get a Job:

Most detectives learn through on the job training, or through a mentor. Only a high school diploma – or less – is required for this job, although some investigators have a background in criminal justice.

If you are hired by a company to investigate fraud, fake disability or insurance claims, or to reconstruct accident scenes, you will go through a training program created by that company.

If you are self-employed, you will typically learn as you go, or through a mentor. You can find professional support by joining the National Association of Legal Investigators or ASIS International (American Society for Industrial Security.)

Loan Officer

- Median yearly wage: $64,660
- Top 10% of earners: **$135,590**
- Typical education: High school diploma
- Additional job requirements: Some have Bachelor's degrees, but not required

What the Job Entails:

Loan Officers are instrumental in the home buying and commercial real estate business. They evaluate, investigate, authorize, and approve loan applications.

Loan Officers talk with potential applicants, usually via phone or email, to get the initial information and records for their applications. They explain the different types of loans and the loan process to the candidate. Most importantly, they gather, analyze, and verify all of the loan applicant's information, especially their financial information, employment information, credit history, and credit score. Lastly, they approve or deny loan applications.

It is the Loan Officer who gauges a candidate's ability to meet the loan criteria and to successfully pay back the loan over a number of years. They also act as a liaison during the process, keeping the candidate informed of where they are in the process, and what information the bank needs from them.

Loan Officers need to have good customer service skills, be able to explain information carefully and patiently, and successfully navigate both the needs and concerns of the candidate and the bank. They spend a significant amount of time managing paperwork, and with digital scanning, that means that they spend a great deal of time in front of a computer, as well.

How to Get a Job:

Many corporate companies expect their loan officers to have professional education, such as a Bachelor's degree in Finance, Business, or Accounting. However, many people who work as loan officers are "grandfathered" in or can start as a File Clerk and gradually work their way up. It is not unheard of for someone to begin working as a temporary employee at a bank or mortgage company, either doing data entry or filing, and over the next few years work their way up to Loan Officer.

Loan Officers receive significant on-the-job training – either through a company training program or through shadowing someone who already has the job.

Corporate programs also typically sponsor their employees through the training process. If you wish to become a Mortgage Loan Officer, you must have a Mortgage Loan Originator license. This involves completing twenty hours of coursework, passing an exam, and going through background and credit checks. A corporate employer may sponsor your way through this program and training.

To get started as a loan officer, begin working in a bank, a credit union, or a mortgage company. You can work your way up through on-the-job training.

Makeup Artist

- Median yearly wage: $25,238
- Top 10% of earners: **$100,000+ for celebrity makeup artists**
- Typical education: High school diploma
- Additional job requirements: Cosmetology license

What the Job Entails:

Makeup artists are typically employed by salons. Many work as independent contractors, working closely with studios, photographers, movie sets, fashion shoots, and individual models. Some makeup artists go on to work in Hollywood, or in major urban areas with a lot of wealthy clientele: New York, San Francisco, Los Angeles, Beverley Hills, San Diego, etc.

Skilled makeup artists may work directly for Hollywood stars, studios, musicians, and photographers.

Makeup artists who specialize in doing makeup for a bride and her bridal party can make a large amount of money in one day.

Famous makeup artists can earn several thousand dollars a day in fees.

Cosmetologists who work in salons may receive large tips from clientele, which supplement their income.

Makeup artists may be employed by fashion and fitness magazines, such as Redbook, Vogue, Oxygen, and Cosmopolitan in order to do work on any variety of models and photo shoots.

Makeup artists may also create or endorse their own line of cosmetics. Examples of this include Bobbi Brown, Alexis Vogel. Creating your own line of cosmetics can lead to a substantial income.

How to Get a Job:

Every state requires that cosmetologists complete a state-licensed program at a cosmetology school. These are small, vocational schools that can be found in most cities. After graduating from school, you must take a state licensing exam. For example, in California, licenses are issued by the California Department of Consumer Affairs Board of Barbering and Cosmetology. Examinations are given Monday through Friday and applicants must have completed a course in cosmetology from a school approved by the Board. The initial cost of a license is $125, with $50 for a renewal.
Once you are licensed, you begin applying to work.

If you wish to work in fashion makeup, you can begin applying to work with photographers, fashion magazines, modeling agencies, and film and television studios.

As a makeup artist, you can always apply to the makeup counters of high-end and upscale department stores. They are an excellent place to gain entry-level skills and experience; all of the clientele comes directly to you.

To work in a beauty salon, look up reputable salons and spas in your area and ask if they are hiring.

If you want to work weddings, begin reaching out to wedding photographers. You will also want to start partnering with hair-stylists who already work on weddings.

You may also want to consider working in the film industry. Special effects artists, who must be especially skilled in makeup, are hired to work on location at film shoots and in Hollywood studios.

Makeup artists are also needed in theater work. They work backstage before the show and inbetween sets to apply makeup to the male and female actors. Some makeup artists travel with large, traveling productions to large cities.

Makeup artists can always find work in New York, Los Angeles, and Hollywood, but if you don't aspire to go to the top of the industry, chances are very good that you can put together a living in your local town by working at a makeup counter or salon, plus doing some weddings on the side.

Military

- Median yearly wage: $32,665
- Top 10% of earners: **$100,000+**
- Typical education: High school
- Additional job requirements: On the job training

What the Job Entails:

The military offers the unique benefit of interesting work where are you pretty much guaranteed regular salary increases, plus the ability to have a lifelong career, if you so choose.

The pay may start off small – but it has the potential to become very generous over time.

A private soldier starts at the lowest salary, around $1,638 a month ($19,656/year.) After three years, his/her salary is up to $2,176 a month ($26,112/year.)

Specialists or corporals start around $2,139 a month ($25,668/year) and go up to $2,596 a month ($31,152/year).

Once a soldier becomes a noncommissioned officer (sergeant or above), they still follow a payscale that begins at $2,332 a month ($27,984/year) and can go as high as $8,033 a month ($96,396/year.)

Soldiers also have the ability to earn extra pay. Soldiers may earn additional hardship pay, special skills pay, foreign language translator pay, or working a position that demands additional responsibility and experience. Soldiers also receive a housing allowance, food allowance, tax advantages, healthcare, and bonuses.

The military is responsible for virtually every aspect of U.S. defense. This means that the military employs soldiers to fight in wars and keep the peace – but they also employ soldiers who work in surprisingly everyday occupations, such as doctors, dentists, nurses, lawyers, office clerks, transcribers, accountants, and receptionists.

Military soldiers engage in defense operations, lead troops, manage personnel, operate vehicles and aircraft, and provide social, physical, medical, and practical support to military personnel.

Soldiers work in combat units to conduct ground operations, maneuver against enemy targets, and operate combat vehicles. Non-combative soldiers may work as building specialists, electrical wiring, computer systems, weapons systems, intelligence planning, work in laboratories, present information, work in food service, repair vehicles, or work in support services. Military careers can be in combat, engineering, administration, health care, human resources, media, emergency management, support services, or transportation. The options are virtually endless.

As of 2017, more than 2.1 million people served in the military. 810,000 more served in the Reserves.

How to Get a Job:

The military has one of the lowest barriers to entry of all career types.

Applicants must be:
- At least 17 years old
- Be a U.S. citizen or have permanent resident status
- Have a high school diploma, GED, or other equivalent
- Have no felony convictions
- Be physically fit
- Pass a medical exam

Some additional requirements must be
- Pass an eye exam
- Gain security clearance
- Unmarried and without children (for some federal service academies)

The military also has age limits. The upper age limit for most branches is age 34. The Coast Guard has a limit of 27, and for the Marine Corps, it is 29. The Air Force accepts the oldest applicants, with a cut-off limit of 39.

Military applicants take a test, called the ASVAB (Armed Forces Vocational Aptitude Battery) to indicate where their specialties and skills are. Soldiers are assigned a specialty based on their aptitude, training, and the needs of their branch.

You may take the ASVAB without a formal commitment to join the military. Many people take the test, then study to increase their score before they make the commitment.

All members of the military sign a contract for the length of their service. Most people enroll for at least four years.

To become an officer in the military, you must typically have a bachelor's degree.

Newly enlisted members undergo basic training, also known as boot camp. It lasts seven to thirteen weeks and is an introduction to the rigors of military life. After basic training, military members go to technical military schools for training in their specialty.

Nuclear Power Reactor Operator

- Median yearly wage: $80,440
- Top 10% of earners: **$108,240**
- Typical education: High school
- Additional job requirements: On the job training, License

What the Job Entails:

Power reactor operators are the employees who control nuclear reactors. They control how much electricity a nuclear reactor generates. They start and stop equipment and record the data associated with the equipment. They monitor and manage reactors, generators, turbines, and cooling systems. They make necessary adjustments and diagnose and resolve any abnormalities.

Nuclear power reactor operators work in control rooms, at a control station. Because power is supplied around the clock, the operator may work the first, second, or third shift.

The job is so high paying because nuclear reactors are dangerous and complex; being an operator means following strict procedures and regulations. Attention to detail is a must for this profession.

How to Get a Job:

Only a high school diploma is required. This job requires extensive on-the-job training. Due to the safety nature of the job, you will also probably need to pass a background check and take regular alcohol and drug tests.

Many people get into this job by climbing up from a lower position, such as a power operator, power dispatcher, or power plant distributor.

To get a license, you will need to take an exam through the US Nuclear Regulatory Commission.

Many companies will also require you to take the Power Plant Maintenance Exam and Plant Operator Exam from Edison Electrical Institute. These are exams that measure spatial ability, mathematical skills, mechanical comprehension, and reading comprehension.

The training the Nuclear Power Reactor Operators undergo is extensive. To become fully qualified, an employee must have undergone several years of training.

To get started, you should apply for an entry-level position at a plant. You can start as an equipment operator or auxiliary operator.

Pilot

- Median yearly wage: $137,330
- Top 10% of earners: **$208,000**
- Typical education: High school education
- Additional job requirements: On the job training

What the Job Entails:

Being a pilot is one of the highest paying professions you can have without a high school diploma.

Commercial pilots do exactly what you would think that they do: they navigate airplanes, and sometimes helicopters.

How to Get a Job:

Commercial pilots need a license from (FAA) Federal Aviation Administration.

In addition to a high school diploma and a license, airlines may require you to meet additional qualifications. You may need certain certificates, instrument ratings, as well as undergoing a health examination, psychological testing, and stress testing.

To become a commercial pilot, you will need to complete training with an independent FAA-certified flight instructor, or attend a school that offers flight training.

While you are training as a commercial pilot, you will accrue many thousands of hours of flight experience. These hours may not be enough to get you a job with an airline, which typically requires 1,500 hours of flying. If you don't already have military flying experience, you can beef up your resume by working as a charter pilot, cargo pilot, crop duster, search and rescue flier, air medical pilot, air tour pilot, or flight instructor.

Once you are hired, you will need to complete on-the-job training as certified by FAR (Federal Aviation Regulations.) This is usually around eight weeks of ground school. You may also need to take more employer training for certification on certain aircraft.

As a commercial pilot, you will also need to undergo ongoing training and submit to regular medical examinations to determine your fitness for flying.

Police Officer

- Median yearly wage: $62,960
- Top 10% of earners: **$105,230**
- Typical education: High school diploma
- Additional job requirements: Police Academy; on the job training

What the Job Entails:

Police officers enforce local, state, and federal laws. They may respond to emergency calls, stop a crime-in-progress, and collect evidence from crime scenes.

Police officers patrol their assigned location, sometimes with a partner. They conduct traffic stops, issue citations and tickets, search vehicle records, detain and arrest suspects, write official reports, and testify in court.

Police officers may work in small or large departments. If it is a large department, they may work in a special unit. Some police officers specialize as a motorcycle cop, horse cop, K9 cop, or as a special weapons officer (SWAT.)

How to Get a Job:

Police candidates have to meet a series of requirements. They must:
- Be at least 21 years old
- Be a U.S. citizen
- Pass a background check
- Pass a drug test
- Must not have a felony conviction
- Must be physically fit

Other requirements:
- May need to pass a vision test
- May need to pass health and psychological testing
- May need to pass a lie detector test

Once a candidate is accepted, they must attend a police academy. Once there, they will go through the academy with a cohort of fellow students. They will receive physical, practical, and classroom training in state and local laws, civil rights, and ethics. They will also study self-defense, take-down tactics, firearms training, first aid, emergency response, and traffic control.

Police officers have room for advancement. After becoming a front-line patrol officer, police officers can go on to supervise or specialize. As they pass more exams, obtain certificates, and gain advanced training, they can promote.

Plumber

- Median yearly wage: $52,590
- **Top 10% of earners: $91,810 (more when working nights, evenings, weekends)**
- Typical education: High school diploma
- Additional job requirements: Licensing

What the Job Entails:

Plumbers work with pipes and septic systems – whether residential, commercial, or industrial. They install, repair, and disassemble pipes which carry gasses, liquids, steam, and sewage. They troubleshoot systems, inspect and test pipes, and determine if pipes conform to local building codes. They work with sanitary drainage, storm drainage, special wastes, vent systems, water systems, and gas piping.

The most well-known plumbers are residential ones. They are called out to the home when the toilet and/or other pipe systems stop working or back up. Plumbers typically work nights, evenings, and weekends – and they charge additional fees for working these non-typical hours.

How to Get a Job:

Most plumbers do not have a formal education in their trade; instead, they learn through an apprenticeship. However, there are trade schools that offer an education in plumbing, pipefitting, and steamfitting.

Apprentices are paid as they learn, getting about 2,000 hours of paid on-the-job training each year. They learn about plumbing codes and regulations, blueprints, and safety. They begin as helpers and assistants, and gain more responsibility as they gain more experience.

To be employed as an apprentice, you must typically meet the following requirements:
- Be at least 18 years old
- Have a high school diploma or a GED
- Be physically fit
- Read, write, and comprehend English
- Must have a valid driver's license
- Be able to present the legal right to work in the United States
- Be able to attend class at least 2 nights a week and perform 2,000 on-the-job hours per year

After completing the apprenticeship program, workers are they promoted to the journey level. That means that they can work on their own. After working for several years, plumbers can take an exam and receive a master status.

Most states require plumbers to have a license and pass an exam demonstrating their knowledge of trade and plumbing codes.

Prison Guard

- Median yearly wage: $51,410
- Top 10% of earners: **$90,880 ($100,000+ with mandatory overtime)**
- Typical education: High school diploma; on-the-job training
- Additional job requirements: Pass a psychological evaluation; special defense training

What the Job Entails:

Prison guards, also known as correctional officers, are the guards who oversee the individuals serving time in prison.

This is a high-conflict job; prison guards are constantly coming into conflict with inmates. Prison guards work either the first, second, or third shift; they also work holidays, weekends, and nights. Guarding a prison is a 24/7 job.

Due to high turnover and shortages in prison guards, many prison guards work overtime. Many have mandatory overtime. The news is full of stories of guards who have *tripled* their salary via overtime. Often, when a prison guard is injured in a confrontation with an inmate, fellow prison guards will be assigned overtime to cover the guard's shift until he/she returns.

Prison guards enforce the rules of the prison and keep inmates from harming themselves and others. They supervise the motions and daily living of the inmates. They search inmates and their physical spaces to check for contraband or weapons. They report on the conduct of inmates and prepare reports and paperwork that document an inmate's poor or dangerous behavior. They are instrumental to preventing assaults, escapes, and attacks. They are frequently called upon to physically restrain, take down, and isolate inmates who prevent a threat.

How to Get a Job:

Like police, correctional officer candidates attend an academy for very specific training on how to do their job.

They will classroom and physical training, followed by on-the-job training at a facility. This training takes several months and may require relocation.

The requirements for acceptance are similar to that of a police officer:
- Be a U.S. citizen
- High school diploma, GED, or equivalent
- At least age 18; some require that you be 21
- For federal prisons, you must have a bachelor's degree OR 1-3 years of full-time work in a field related to counseling or supervision
- By physically fit
- Pass a psychological examination
- No previous felonies
- Eligible to own a firearm

Potential correctional officers go through a selection process. The following characteristics will probably be examined, in addition to a traditional skill set:
- Personal character
- Credit report

- Driving Record
- Legal records search
- Background check
- Personal relationships
- Employment history

Throughout the selection process, you will complete and be scored on the following:
- Written exam
- Physical fitness tests
- Vision test
- Psychological examination
- Medical exam

The time it takes from first applying to getting a prison guard job can be 6 months or more! If you pass all exams, you will be scheduled to attend academy training, then placed at a prison. Be aware before you begin that the work may require you (and your family) to relocate to be close to a prison.

Radiation Therapist

- Median yearly wage: $80,570
- Top 10% of earners: **$123,020**
- Typical education: Certificate program
- Additional job requirements: Licensing

What the Job Entails:

Radiation therapists work in a variety of environments – most often hospitals, but also outpatient facilities and doctor's offices. They give radiation treatments to patients in order to combat cancer and other diseases.

Radiation therapists help manage patient care from the beginning to end of treatment. They explain to the patient what the treatment will be, how it will proceed, when it will end, and they also answer any questions the patient may have. They help the patient prepare for the treatment and ensure that they will not be exposed to an improper amount of radiation. They position the patient for treatment, operate the machine that performs the radiation treatment, and monitors the patient during treatment. They also enter patient information and keep detailed records of the treatment plan.

Radiation therapists must be able to manage the radiation equipment with procession while still managing the emotional needs of the patient.

How to Get a Job:

Many radiation therapists have a two-year degree in radiation therapy, but many more radiation therapists met the requirement for a position just by attending a certificate program.

The education that you will receive in a certificate program will have practical courses in a clinical setting. You will study radiation techniques, human anatomy and physiology, radiation oncology, treatment planning, treatment delivery, and patient care.

Some positions may also require that you know CPR.

After attending a certificate program, radiation therapists must pass licensing or certification. Licensing requirements vary state by state. They must also adhere to the ethical standards of the American Registry of Radiologic Technologists.

To get started, you will want to enroll in a radiation therapist program. Candidates who have prior or current work experience in a medical setting will find it easier to get into a program and to find work afterward. Consider getting a position as a nursing assistant or as a caregiver while you prepare for your certification.

Real Estate Appraiser

- Median yearly wage: $54,010
- Top 10% of earners: **$101,710**
- Typical education: High school diploma or equivalent (for entry-level state license)
- Additional job requirements: Certification

What the Job Entails:

Appraisers value real estate property.

They record the details, properties, and characteristics of a particular property and its surrounding area. They appraise the condition of a building, photograph the interior and exterior of the building, note any potential problems that would cause a decrease in value, and make notes on the property. After visiting the property in person, they value the property against other properties in the area. Appraisers may research recent home sales, compare housing prices for a particular geographical region, and then give an estimate on that particular property's financial value.

Appraisers work locally, appraise only one property at a time, and may appraise either new or existing property as well as commercial and residential property.

How to Get a Job:

Many appraisers now have a Bachelor's degree, but it is still possible to become an appraiser working with a small company or with some college. The entry-level licensing category usually goes not require that you have a bachelor's degree. In some areas, you only need a high school diploma. Check with your state's licensing board for specific requirements for an appraiser.

Appraisers must have excellent organizational, research, and data skills. They will check legal records and document on a property, and keep excellent records on their observations in order to justify their valuation of a property.

An employer may send you to basic appraisal courses, or provide you with on-the-job training and mentorship with an experienced appraiser.

Real Estate Broker

- Median yearly wage: $56,730
- Top 10% of earners: **$151,660**
- Typical education: High school diploma or equivalent
- Additional job requirements: Certification

What the Job Entails:

Everyone knows someone who is making a great living in real estate!

Real estate brokers and sales agents help clients buy, sell, and rent properties.

Most real estate brokers and sales agents are self-employed. Although they often work irregular hours, many are able to set their own schedules.

What do real estate brokers do?

In short: they buy and sell properties. They work one-on-one with clients to take them to see properties for sell, and advise them on the price, potential mortgage, and the flavor of the neighborhood. They are knowledgeable about the details of each property; the location, the features, any special history of the property. They help the buyer create a purchase offer and submit it to the seller; they negotiate between the buyer and seller. They help the buyer understand the terms of the purchase and all legal contracts; they may also work with the seller.

A real estate broker may either assist the buyer or the seller. They may also help to rent or manage properties.

How to Get a Job:

Every state requires real estate brokers and agents to be licensed. Requirements vary by state but generally require candidates to be at least 18 years old, complete a number of hours of real estate or college courses, and pass a licensing exam.

Real estate brokers and sales agents must complete some real estate courses to be eligible for licensure. Although most brokers and agents must take state-accredited pre-licensing courses to become licensed, some states may waive this requirement if the candidate has taken college courses in real estate.

Candidates must:
- be 18 years old
- complete a number of real estate courses
- pass an exam

Some states have additional requirements, such as passing a background check.

Researcher

- Median yearly wage: $54,270
- Top 10% of earners: **$100,660**
- Typical education: High school
- Additional job requirements: Database and online searching skills

What the Job Entails:

Researchers work on a wide variety of projects. They may do any of the following:
- Genealogical research and family trees
- Census searches
- Court record searches
- Vital records search (birth, marriage, and death certificates)
- Lands records search
- Property owner search
- Title and deed search
- Cemetery records
- Historical research (newspaper articles, etc.)
- Informational research
- Competitor research
- Skip tracing (debtor or fugitive recovery)
- Missing persons

Projects may vary wildly; most people end up developing a specialty.

Some of the most popular types of research are genealogical and skip tracing.

Genealogical research can take an enormous amount of time and money. Interested parties may want copies of birth, marriage, divorce, and death records. They may want someone to search Ancestry.com for them or go to a cemetery and get a photo of their great-grandfather's headstone. They may want to know the history of a relative's property and need a search done on land records, or maps of the local area from two hundred years ago.

Once a client has made an investment in genealogical research, a project could take hundreds of hours before they have a complete family tree. Researchers can be paid for their time, mileage, and copying fees as they visit county clerk offices and archives.

Another popular research field is skip tracing, also known as debt recovery, fugitive recovery, or bounty hunting. Glamorized and popularized in movies and TV shows, much of the work involved in skip tracing is far from glamorous. Skip tracers are employed by debt collectors, bail bondmen, process servers, repossession agents, private detectives, lawyers, journalists, and private individuals. The skip tracer's job is to collect information on the fugitive and locate their current whereabouts. To do so, they access phone records, credit reports, background checks, utility records, and public information, such as tax information. In some cases, the skip tracer isn't able to local the fugitive, but can successfully locate associates of the fugitive, and a history of where the fugitive has been living and working.

Sadly, another growing field is the missing persons field. Thousands of adults go voluntarily missing each year. The growing opioid epidemic has made many adults abandon their homes, their families, their jobs, and their lifestyles. Concerned parents are willing to pay thousands of dollars if you can locate their missing adult child so that they can be found and receive treatment.

How to Get a Job:

Many people who have Master's degrees and PhD's and who haven't been successful in finding lucrative work enter this field, but don't let that intimidate you. This is a field where *results* matter more than credentials. You are either able to find the information that the client is looking for, or you don't. While having an advanced degree may help you build more impressive credentials to attract new clients, you can not have a degree and let your portfolio speak for itself!

To learn research skills, I have several suggestions:
- Read *The Extreme Searcher's Internet Handbook: A Guide for the Serious Searcher* by Randolph Hock
- Reads books on how to locate missing persons, such as: *How to Find Missing Persons: A Handbook for Investigators* by Ronald Eriksen and *How to Find Almost Anyone, Anywhere* by Norma Mott Tillman

- Visit your local public library, county library, law library, state library, university library, archives, local history center, city clerk's office, county recorder's office, and courthouse, familiarize yourself with their resources
- Familiarize yourself with reverse cell phone lookup sites, reverse address websites, and public information lookup sites

To start skip tracing, you will need to build a website. Many clients will find you over the internet and submit their inquiries via email. Make sure that you give the client a realistic timeline; at least two weeks or 10 business days for you to conduct your search. Bill by the hour and be prepared to send the client an invoice on all of the work that you have done in searching, even if not all leads were successful.

Sales Manager

- Median yearly wage: $121,060
- Top 10% of earners: **$208,000**
- Typical education: High school
- Additional job requirements: N/A

What the Job Entails:

Sales managers are responsible for directing a staff of salespeople. They set selling goals, motivate salespeople, and report sales statistics and information to management.

Working in sales an excellent job for extroverts. Why? Because some of the most common situations you will be dealing with are:
- Resolving customer complaints and issues
- Monitoring customer behavior and salesmen behavior to ensure that sales are going well
- Maximizing the potential of sales staff to ensure that the most and best sales are made
- Approve special discounts and pricing
- Set sales quotas
- Determine sales territories
- Study local markets and sales statistics to maximize sales projections
- Hire and interview new staff
- Train and incentivize staff
- Let underperforming staff go

Sales managers typically have a territory that they are responsible for. They made work on site, or rotate between several sites to ensure the maximization of sales at each one.

They also meet one-on-one with sales staff members to go over sales goals and to discuss individual performance. Staff who are not meeting and exceeding sales quota are typically let go.

Sales managers may work in two different types of sales: B2B and B2C.

B2B stands for business-to-business sales. These are sales from one business to another. For example, a manufacturer may sell to a wholesales, and a wholesaler may sell to retail stores. In this case, the customer is another company.

B2C stands for business-to-consumer sales. These are sales between a business to a customer. Think of a retail store, a department store, an electronics company, or an auto dealership.

How to Get a Job:

You will find it easiest to work in sales if you are available on evenings and weekends. Many sales jobs are in retail stores and auto dealerships.

A sales manager must work their way up; they have a proven track record as a sales person.

It is easy to start working in sales, especially if you are commission based. That means that if you don't sell anything, you don't make any money. Auto dealerships and print publications such as newspapers and local magazines are almost hiring commission-only salespeople.

When you are hired as a salesperson, your training will be on-the-job. You will start out making cold calls and visits to potential clients. Desirable traits are:
- A thick skin
- Persistence
- The ability to negotiate
- Excellent communication skills
- Empathy
- Excellent organizational skills
- Preparation

As you just start out, you will make many cold calls. You need to be prepared with materials about the product you are selling and convince the client that they should listen to you long enough for you to present your product.

If you are successful in sales, you will find yourself rapidly promoted, as the turnover in sales is so high. After a few years of promotions, you should be able to reach the sales manager level.

Skycap

- Median yearly wage: $23,230
- Top 10% of earners: **$100,000**
- Typical education: High school education
- Additional job requirements: N/A

What the Job Entails:

Skycaps, also known as curbside porters, are the curbside workers at airports who assist you with your luggage. They work at the airport curb, taking bags from travelers and checking them in for their flights. They also use dollies and carts to help customers with large amounts of luggage.

Skycaps do not actually work for an airline – they are contractors.

Skycaps earn good wages through quantity – not quality. Handling a lot of bags can lead to a lot of tips. Typically, they earn some sort of minimum wage through the contractor. Their real wealth comes through the small cash tips that they collect from customers.

A good skycap can have a lifelong career at a busy airport and make very good money – up to $100,000 a year.

These are some rough guidelines to what you may earn as a skycap:
- A single bag: $1-2
- Multiple bags: $5
- Heavy bags: $5

- Helping a customer who is late for a flight: $5-10
- Assisting in transporting a customer in a wheelchair or helping a parent with a stroller all the way to the gate: $10-20

How to Get a Job:

To get a job, you will need to apply to a contractor who works with the airlines. You will be employed by the contractor, not the airline itself.

Skycaps undergo a very short amount of on-the-job training.

Be aware that this is physical and uncomfortable work. You will be on the curb 8 hours a day – whether it's raining, snowing, or in blazing heat.

You will be handling large, physically heavy bags. Customers may be rude, irritable, stressed, and refuse to tip.

You will also be expected to work nights, weekends, and holidays.

Small Business Owner

- Median yearly wage: $59,491
- Top 10% of earners: **$150,000+**
- Typical education: High school diploma
- Additional job requirements:

What the Job Entails:

If you're a small business owner, you're in good company. Here are some statistics about small businesses:

- There are 29 million+ small businesses in the U.S.
- Over 50% of the working population works in a small business
- 80% of these businesses have no employers – meaning they are sole proprietorships, and they are owned by a single person
- Small businesses generate 3/5 of new jobs
- 52% of all small businesses are home-based
- Approximately **543,000 new businesses** get started **each month**
- **As a small business, you must have business receipts of $1,000+ a year to pay federal income taxes**
- **Small businesses have average revenues of $44,000**
- 7 out of 10 new businesses make it the least two years
- 5 out of 10 new businesses make it at least 5 years
- 4 out of 10 new businesses make it at least 10 years
- 3 out of 10 news businesses make it at least 15 years

Small business owners work in every field. Some examples would be:
- Retail
- Bookkeeping
- Automotive
- Marketing
- Home inspection
- Fitness or wellness
- Hairdressing/makeup
- Graphic design
- Restaurants
- Food trucks
- Catering
- Wedding photographer
- Copywriter
- Cleaning and janitorial
- Security

If you're just starting a small business, I would recommend that you start with something you know. If you wanted to buy a business right out of the box, you could always be a franchise owner.

There are a lot of advantages to running your own small business:
- Be your own boss
- Set your own hours
- Work when you want

You will spend most of your time:

- Advertising your business
- Doing social media for your business
- Managing the paperwork associated with your business
- Providing customer service
- Marketing your product and figuring out how to sell more

Their primary duties (outside of their respective skill or trade) include managing employees, providing customer service, promoting their business, filing and documenting appropriate business accounts, and ensuring their business meets any local, state, and federal requirements. Small business owners may work from a storefront, office space, or even from their home. Depending on the type of business, trade, or service they practice, their hours can vary; however, many organizations operate during daytime hours.

- Oversee company operations, directing production, sales, administrative, and/or distribution activities.
- Oversee and/or assist with personnel management, including hiring, training, and performance evaluation.
- Oversee and/or assist with client acquisition and marketing strategies.
- Develop and/or assist with company-wide policies, procedures, objectives, and business strategies.
- Direct and review financial activities, measuring productivity, setting prices, and/or managing budgets.

Tattoo Artist

- Median yearly wage: $30,000
- Top 10% of earners: **$114,380**
- Typical education: High school education
- Additional job requirements: Apprenticeship

What the Job Entails:

Tattoo artists have been popularized by reality TV shows like *Bad Ink*, *Ink Master*, and *LA Ink*.

The reality of being a tattoo artist can be far less glamorous than a show depicts, but it is still a very cool job. For the most part, you get to set your own hours, work as much or as little as you want, and do creative and independent work.

As a tattoo artist, you will apply permanent artwork to skin by using needles and ink.

There are two kinds of shops: walk-in and custom. Some shops are a combination of the two. In a walk-in shop, a customer can come in, pick a design off the wall, and get a tattoo immediately. Their tattoo may take a few hours, at most, and that may be the only work that you do for them. In a custom shop, you will work with customers in advance to plan and create elaborate, custom-made designs. You develop relationships with your customers, and may work with them for many months or years. In a custom shop, you will do some of your most creative work.

There are three steps to creating a custom tattoo:

- Meeting one-on-one with a client to discuss their vision
- Sketching the tattoo
- Designing and redesigning until the client is satisfied

In addition to doing new tattoos on clean skin, you may also be called to cover old tattoos and reworking bad tattoos or prison tattoos.

After you have gained experience in the field, you may want to open your own shop. Being a shop owner is like any other business. You will be responsible for:
- Hiring and firing
- All paperwork/invoicing
- Insurance
- Hiring cleaning staff or cleaning the studio
- Scheduling
- Resolving customer service issues and problems
- Promoting your shop

Just be aware that as a shop owner, you may spend more time resolving customer service issues and other issues with your shop than you will doing tattoos.

How to Get a Job:

Tattooing is like any other art. Tattoo artists are commissioned to create art for a client. Your art just happens to be on the body. To be in this field, you need to be artistically talented, although you don't need an art education or an art degree.

Tattoo artists either work for another artist who owns the shop, or they work independently and run their own shop. As a beginning tattoo artist, you will start out working for another shop. When working for another tattoo artist, you will typically either rent a chair/station from the owner, or be a part of the shop staff but earn 40-50% commission on the cost of the tattoo.

You will start you tattoo career as an apprentice, or a trainee artist. In most cases, this is an unpaid apprenticeship. You will work the first 1-2 years for free. At first, you won't be able to tattoo at all. You will help run the shop. Some of your tasks may be: cleaning the studio, scheduling appointments, preparing the tattoo stations of other artists, doing promotion. In the beginning, the tattoos you will be doing will be of very simple designs.

You will also need to pay for your own equipment. To start, you will need two tattoo machines, a ink set, tubes, needles, gloves, rubberbands, transfer paper, skin pens, etc. You will also need to pay state licensing fees.

After several years of practice, you will have accumulated a portfolio of your work, which will allow you to gain more clients, work independently, and eventually open your own shop.

UPS Driver

- Median yearly wage: $76,955
- Top 10% of earners: **$100,000+**
- Typical education: High school
- Additional job requirements: UPS Academy (paid training)

What the Job Entails:

UPS, or the United Parcel Service, delivers more than 15 million packages a day. They employ part-time, seasonal, and full-time workers. Their full-time, permanent workers have some of the best benefits in private industry – if you're willing to stick with the company long enough to get them.

The real benefit of working with UPS comes with the overtime.

UPS's top hourly rate is $34/hour. Overtime occurs after 8 hours of work. Many drivers work 12 hour shifts each day.

In addition to the high pay, UPS driver typically enjoy great benefits: free health insurance, dental insurance, vision insurance, tuition assistance, paid vacation and sick leave, and a retirement pension after 30 years.

On the downside, you can be on call 24/7 as a UPS driver.

Drivers carry handheld computers that track their moves and their time efficiency. Drivers may make between 150 to 200 stops per day – and every one of his or her movements during that delivery is timed.

New drivers go through specialized training classes that mimic real driving and delivery scenarios.

Drivers learn how to safely handle heavy packages, how to drive the truck, how to walk and carry packages in all weather conditions, include rain and snow.

How to Get a Job:

Most UPS employees start off as a part-time, seasonal package handler. This is a way to get a foot in the door.

UPS primarily employees for two different types of jobs: package handler and driver.

Package handlers are just as they sound. They sort and pack packages. These jobs are frequently part-time and are filled by people deliberately looking to work part-time, or for serious future employees trying to make a career with UPS and who are trying to get their foot in the door.

The drivers are responsible for delivering all the packages. They drive regular routes, and timed and monitored on their driving, and are expected to be quick, efficient, and physically fit. Packages typically weigh between 25 and 65 pounds. You will also need to have an excellent driving record and will need to get a commercial driver's license.

UPS drivers, regardless of whether they are package handlers or drivers, must pass a physical exam to ensure that they are fit enough to handle the packages.

Like most jobs now, you will need to apply online. Through the UPS website, you will start an employment profile that includes your personal and contact information. You will also need to include references.

Even if your goal is to work for UPS full-time, consider applying for seasonal, part-time positions. This is an easy way to gain experience with UPS and get your foot in the door.

If there are positions open, you will be contacted for an interview. Because of the popularity of UPS jobs, there are many interviewees for each job.

You can watch mock interviews on the UPS website to increase your interview skills.

During the interview, you will be asked about your physical abilities and your potential ability to handle packages (again, lifting 65 or more pounds.)

If you are hired by UPS, expect that you will need to work your way up in seniority and pay, and it may be several years before you cross the six-figure mark.

USPS Postal Worker

- Median yearly wage: $57,260
- Top 10% of earners: **$100,000+ overtime**
- Typical education: High school diploma
- Additional job requirements: On-the-job training

What the Job Entails:

Being a USPS postal worker is a job that can get you to six figures – but not without significant overtime.

The top pay for being a city mail carrier will get you up to $60,000-$70,000 a year. With overtime, it is possible to break six figures. With Mondays being typically busy, and lots of extra work around the holidays, it is possible to get significant overtime if you work for a busy office.

Postal workers typically work in one of three different tracks: mail sorter, mail carrier, or postal clerk.

Mail sorters do the following:
- Sort incoming mail, including letters and packages
- Operate postal equipment and machinery
- Receive mail from large postal trucks
- Pack mail and package for outgoing delivery

Mail carriers do the following:
- Pick up letters and packages
- Deliver mail to homes and businesses
- Walk and drive along established routes in rural, suburban, or city areas

Postal clerks work in a retail location (a USPS counter or office) and do the following:
- Assist customers with sending domestic and international mail
- Help customers decide how their package should be shipped
- Answer basic questions about mail service
- Collect change-of-address cards
- Assist customers with mail that requires signatures, or which has been held by the USPS
- Sell stamps and other post-office related items, such as cards, tape, and packaging
- Sell money orders
- Help customers begin or stop service for a postal box

How to Get a Job:

To work for USPS, you need to meet the following qualifications:
- US citizenship
- Must be at least 18 years old
- Or, must be at least 16 years old with a diploma
- High school diploma or equivalent education
- Pass a drug test
- Pass a criminal background check

To be a mail carrier, there are additional requirements:
- Have driver's license
- Have a good driving record
- Be able to lift 50 pounds and pass a physical exam
- Be able to walk 10 or more miles a day

To get started applying for USPS, visit the Careers section of the USPS website. The USPS website has helpful instructions and FAQ's for applying. They recommend that you set aside at least two hours to complete the entire online application process.

You will need to create an account on the USPS website; basically, you will be creating an online application. You will fill out your personal information, your education experience, your work experience, and your qualifications.

After filling out the application, you can apply for jobs. Some applicants will receive an e-mail invitation to take an assessment. Many jobs also have limits on how many applicants can apply. For example, only the first 50 applicants may apply. If you were not a part of the first 50, you won't receive an invite to take the assessment.

Once you are invited to take an assessment, known as the Postal Exam 473, you have 7 days to complete the assessment process. You must establish an assessment account. After completing that, you will receive further emails with requests for information and to complete further steps in the process.

One of these further steps is a 90-minute online assessment. Once that assessment is completed, you may be invited to attend an in-person, proctored exam. This will also take up to 90 minutes and will be done at a computer at an authorized locations with authorized personnel. You will receive emailed instructions about what you need to bring to the Test Center.

If you plan to be a mail carrier, you will also need to pass a physical examination to ensure that you meet the job requirements. Mail carriers have the most physically intensive job, as they must deliver mail in all weather conditions. They deal with natural hazards: icy roads, icy sidewalks, blizzard, rainstorms, and extremely hot temperatures. They must also deal with other hazards, such as hostile customers and dangerous dogs.

Once you pass and complete a background check, you can begin applying for positions.

Waiter

- Median yearly wage: $20,820
- Top 10% of earners: **$100,000+**
- Typical education: None
- Additional job requirements: None

What the Job Entails:

Waiters and waitresses work in restaurants, hotels, bars, wine bars, bistros, chain restaurants, and specialty dining rooms. They work very closely with the public to serve them and to create a satisfying dining experience.

They greet customers as they enter the serving area or are seated at a table, present them with menus and wine lists, and recite the daily specials. They must have the menu memorized, and be able to answers any questions related to the menu or the drink list. After answering questions about the menu and the specials, the waiter or waitress takes the order and suggests wine pairings, appetizers, or other recommendations.

After taking the order, the waiter's job is to convey the order to the kitchen staff, including any adjustments or substitutions. They bring out the food and drink orders, check in with the customers, remove and box uneaten foods, clear dishes, take payments, and may also be responsible for resolving minor disputes over the bill.

Waiters in fine dining restaurants may end up serving a customer over the course of several hours; several courses and different wines are a common part of the dining experience. Given the exclusive nature of the restaurant, the waiter is also tasked with making the customer feel as if they have received excellent personal attention and the very best of service.

Waiters need to be prepared to deal with demanding customers, other waiters and waitresses, and a large kitchen staff. No matter how busy or demanding the job, a waiter in a fine dining establishment must appear cool, calm, unrushed, and competent.

Fine dining establishments have strict requirements for appearance. Waiters and waitresses are expected to wear either black or white, to be well groomed, to keep jewelry small and discreet, and to hide any tattoos or piercings. Fine dining establishments may have specific uniforms or aprons.

Although some technical colleges offer degrees in food service, a high school degree is usually adequate to get a position. Most states require workers who serve alcoholic beverages to be at least 18 years of age. Some states require you to get a special license to serve alcohol.

How to Get a Job:

Most waiters and waitresses learn through short-term on-the-job training. No previous education or experience is required for casual eateries and diners. Fine dining, fine hotel restaurants, bistros, and upscale restaurants employ more experienced staff.

Many chain restaurants are always hiring to cover their extended open hour. If you are willing to work weekends and late nights, you are likely to be hired.

Your first few days on the job can be jarring. Before your first day, be sure to inquire about what you are expected to wear or if there is a uniform. You might try carrying a large stack of heavy books around your home – this will give you good practice for balancing a large and heavy tray.

On your first day, wear comfortable shoes. Consider shoes that have good traction or are non-slip, as you will likely be watching across the kitchen area, where the floor is frequently wet. Wear pants with pockets. Bring several pens for customers to sign credit cards receipts with. Remember to balance cold plates on your arm, and put the hot plates on a serving tray. If you must carry a hot plate on your arm, drape a towel over it first. Bring small bills - $1's and $5's – to provide change to customers or to break large bills for customers. Also bring coins.

Wedding Photographer

- Median yearly wage: $62,135
- Top 10% of earners: **$100,000+**
- Typical education: High school degree
- Additional job requirements: A digital camera

What the Job Entails:

Clients expect their photos to be digital – they expect to be handed a CD, flash drive, or be given access to a digital album after the wedding. While some photographers may specialize in using special print film for weddings, these will be few and far between. Most clients want and expect the convenience of a CD – not a book of print and negatives to go with it. In many geographic areas, there are now no longer any stores or photo shops that are capable of processing print film. Major cities like New York and Los Angeles may have several photo studios and specialty camera shops that can accommodate print film, but not any rural areas. So expect to shoot digitally and give your customers a digital product.

With this job, you will need to have a certain amount of culture sensitivity. You may be photographing weddings that are Catholic, Protestant, Baptist, Orthodox Jewish, non-denominational, and even Wiccan, such as a handfasting ceremony. You may be marrying male-female couples, or male-male and female-female couples. Your clients may be culturally and socioeconomically diverse. Their behavior may also vary, too. You may privately wonder why a bride is marrying a drunk, loud man who is idiotically bragging about what he did at his bachelor party, but it's up to you to continue on as professionally as possible.

People experience a wide-range of emotions at their wedding. It's up to you to capture the funny moments, the teary moments, the joyous moments. You'll want couples to look back at their wedding album years later, look at the emotions in their eyes, and think: *yes, that's why I married this person.*

As a photographer, it's your job to be in many places at once – without being intrusive. Be aware that in some culture, you may also need to be sensitive about where you are in relation to the wedding party. For example, in a Catholic ceremony, it is not appropriate for you to on level with the alter.

How to Get a Job:

Many wedding photographers have a degree in photography, but this is another job where results matter more than credentials.

Be aware that there should be more than just you on the job, however. You will need a backup photographer, and maybe even a lighting assistant, for each wedding. That's because while you are doing the formal, posed shots with the bride and groom, you will need a second photographer to capture all the casual, offbeat moments while you are otherwise occupied. The lighting assistant is for the outdoor shots – they will need to redirect silver sheets and extra lights to make sure the wedding party is appropriately lit in the shots.

If you aren't good at digital editing, you may need to hire one more assistant to enhance the shots afterward.

Wedding photographers charge in one of two ways: by the hour, and a flat fee. If you charge a flat fee, you need to decide on a minimum number of hours that you will be at each wedding. For example, some weddings may go five or six hours, and others only two. You may need to guarantee clients that you will be there a minimum amount of time, such as two to three hours.

Get your start by running an advertisement in a local magazine. Many major cities have "lifestyle" magazines or even put an annual or semi-annual wedding issue for brides. You should also consider getting a booth at any bridal expos or events in your area.

Another way to get the word out about your business is to start making connections with others in the bridal industry. Visit local salons, hairdressers, nail salons, spas, and makeup artists and ask if you can leave your business cards with them. You may also consider offering them a referral fee – if they recommend you to photograph someone's wedding and you are booked, you will pay them a fee.

YouTube Entrepreneur

- Median yearly wage: $30
- Top 10% of earners: $1,001
- **Top 1% of earners: $1 million+**
- Typical education: High school or above
- Additional job requirements: None

What the Job Entails:

YouTube Entrepreneurs are self-employed creative types who make, edit, and upload their own videos to YouTube. YouTube allows you to become an instant expert in almost any field by either providing tutorials or entertainment for the masses.

Do you know how to do HAM radio? Start a YouTube channel for amateurs interested in getting their license.

Want to teach women how to do their hair or makeup? Start a tutorial channel.

Have a pet that does adorable things? Think your cat or Chihuahua could be an instant internet star? Upload videos.

Want to teach skateboard tricks? Upload.

Teach algebraic equations? Upload.

You get the message.

To make money off of YouTube, you need to be at the very top. 90% of YouTube channels don't make more than $2.50 a month and receive about 400 views per month. Most of the bottom YouTube channels make less than $100 a year. Income is paid out at an estimated $1 per 1,000 views.

If you reach the top 3.5%, or at least one million views per month, your annual advertising revenue will be $12,000 to $16,000 a year. The top 3% of channels account for 63% of all the viewings on YouTube.

The good news is that the numbers of channels which earn $100,000+ a year grows about 40% each year. This is reflective of the overall growth of YouTube.

The top 1% of YouTube creators have between 2 million and 42 million views per month. In addition to getting revenue through YouTube, these creators often negotiate sponsorships and other contracts that bring in additional income.

As of this writing, there are some of the most successful YouTube vloggers, with estimated salaries ranging from $5 million to $15 million a year:
- PewDiePie – (gamer) 54 million subscribers
- German Garmendia (comedian, musician) 31.2 million subscribers
- Smosh (parodies, pop culture) 22.6 million subscribers
- Yuya (beauty, hair, makeup) 17.8 million subscribers

- DudePerfect (sports comedy) 16.2 million subscribers
- JennaMarbles (comedic videos aimed at Millennials) 16.9 million subscribers
- Jacksepticeye – (gamer) 14.8 million subscribers
- DanTDM – (Minecraft gamer) 14.4 million subscribers

How to Get a Job:

YouTube has one of the lowest barriers to entry. You can simply sign up for an account and start loading videos.

Since YouTube users can watch videos for free, how do you make money? Your earnings come through YouTube's Partner Program. YouTube content creators – or vloggers (video bloggers) earn money through the advertisements that are played before their videos.

Generally, the amount paid out per advertisement if very small, but your revenues will increase as your channel gains more popularity and subscribers.

How do you get into the Partner Program? New channels require at least 1,000 channel subscribers and 4,000 hours of viewed material over a 1-year period.

The biggest challenge to being a YouTube start is getting noticed. Every minute, more than 400 hours of video are uploaded to YouTube. The site also has 1.5 billion monthly users.

If you want to increase your odds of success, start a video game channel. Gamer vloggers have a fourteen times higher chance of getting subscribers than traditional vloggers.

www.ingramcontent.com/pod-product-compliance
Lightning Source LLC
Chambersburg PA
CBHW030945240526
45463CB00016B/1959